BALLASTED
WINGS

Why That Day?

BALLASTED WINGS

Why That Day?

SUSAN KNOX KOPTA

ISBN: 978-1-4834-2952-6 (sc)
ISBN: 978-1-4834-2951-9 (e)

Image 1 was edited by Elizabeth Ming Cooper, emcooperfineart.com
Image 3 is by Bonnie Vculek, facebook.com/bonnie.vculek

Columbia Daily Spectator, Volume CXXX, Number 59, 19 April 2006: "BC Senior Killed in Car Wreck: Alexis 'Lexie' Knox, 22, was a Well-Known Campus Face" by Kira Goldenberg (Chapter 27, p. 107) was reproduced with permission from Spectator Publishing, Co.

Lulu Publishing Services rev. date: 01/13/2020

Disclaimer, Warnings & Resources

DISCLAIMER: *Ballasted Wings: Why That Day?* is based primarily on facts. However, my recall is not entirely clear. Nor was I privy to many conversations. Some names, places and descriptions are changed to protect privacy. Statements made regarding bipolar and suicide reflect my observations, interpretations and lay opinions. Alexis's bipolar events largely occurred in late 2005 through early 2006 and reflect circumstances of that time.

WARNING: This book is not intended as a substitute for medical or other professional advice. Consult qualified professionals, including your treating physician/psychiatrist and other licensed medical care professionals for mental and physical health matters.

TRIGGER WARNING: This book addresses topics some may find disturbing including suicide. If you have suicidal ideations, are suicidal or prone to suicide in any way, do not read this book as it could be a trigger.

SUICIDE PREVENTION: If you are in suicide crisis, call 911 and/or the *National Suicide Prevention Lifeline*: **800-273-8255** (TALK).

BIPOLAR RESOURCES: If you need a hub for bipolar resources including supplemental suicide prevention resources see *BipolarLinks.com*, created by the author.

Alexis

Reading Time

Approximately Fifty-five Minutes

Dedicated to

Alexis Geneva Knox

Alexis: Ballasted Wings

. . . we know what we are but know not what we may be.

— William Shakespeare, *Hamlet*
Ophelia (4.5.43)

Targeted Audience

The primary target audience for *Ballasted Wings: Why That Day?* is

- mental health caregivers
- mental health advocates
- those directly affected by bipolar
- family, friends and loved ones of those with bipolar

This book is *not* intended for persons with bipolar who

o   are not stabilized;
o   are not in treatment; or
o   are suicidal

CONTENTS

SOARS

Chapter 1

*A*lexis's wings lack ballast. She soars too fast. She flies too high. She lands too hard. She plunges below the surface. She flies without balance, but she flies.

Alexis achieves, achieves, achieves so much in our rural town. Science fair awards, first chair oboe, a page for the Oklahoma Senate, outstanding French student in junior high and high school. First in her school to travel abroad to *be* a foreign exchange student.

Alexis is chosen for early admission into Barnard College of Columbia University, a prestigious women's college in New York City. Alexis arrives and chooses two areas for academic concentration: women's studies and human rights. Even among the highly qualified student body, Alexis is selected as a potential Centennial Scholar.

Outside academics, Alexis serves on the Sexual Misconduct Committee. Alexis fights for change; for justice. She twice receives a Student Government Leadership award.

Alexis advocates on behalf of professors as well as classmates. The *Columbia Daily Spectator* runs a front-page article on a hearing involving tenure for Barnard and Columbia professors. It features a photograph of Alexis as she speaks passionately to support the rights of female professors.

Barnard holds its annual Mentor Walk. Alexis is paired with the corporate sponsor's CEO. She and Alexis lead the walk. Fists raised.

Off campus, Alexis volunteers. She is an advocate for domestic violence survivors at *Sanctuary for Families*. She interns for Senator Hillary Clinton.

Alexis works for Ms. Gloria Steinem at the *Ms. Foundation for Women*. Amy Richards, author and founder of *Third Wave*, supervisors her. Ms. Richards describes Alexis as the epitome of a Barnard student.

Alexis soars.

SWAYS

Chapter 2

*A*lexis loves her young adult college life. A life built on hard work, passion and the wings of mania. She wants to maintain that manic energy so to create, to fulfill dreams, to soar.

Her goal? To fly without the crash. To keep long hours without exhaustion. To ride mania's unbridled enthusiasm without encountering overwhelming commitments.

Alexis's goal proves unattainable. While riding mania's wave, euphoric creativity brings an avalanche of ideas. Abundant enthusiasm colors her judgment. She loses concept of limitations; of the need for sleep.

Then, dysfunctional valves open to a flow of dark depression. An undertow of despair dilutes, weakens, obliterates excess energy. Mania washes away.

Alexis is slung between manic and depressive cycles. She sways uncontrollably on ropes of yet-to-be-diagnosed bipolar. She tries therapy but feels it is not helping.

One day, Alexis takes the bus to her therapy session but does not attend. She lacks emotional energy to engage. She seeks ballast elsewhere.

Alexis finds a tattoo studio. Desperately, she has an anchor tattooed on each ankle.

Alas, she is not anchored.

PSYCHOSIS

Chapter 3

*I*n the throes of bipolar depression, desire, energy and motivation are elusive. Alexis needs a boost, a lift, an elevation. She reaches through depression's dark abyss to grasp manic energy. Her grip too weak.

An acquaintance calls. She's just been released from drug rehab and is in need of a place to sleep. The One-in-Need claims she has no one else to call.

Alexis knows not what to do. She provides the One-in-Need her apartment address. The One-in-Need arrives. She offers Alexis heroin. Alexis declines and retreats under depression's blanket.

A body atop. Alexis struggles. Her arm imprisoned, reddens and swells. The One-in-Need muscle pops Alexis with heroin.

Within minutes Alexis relaxes, goes limp, detaches. The One-in-Need injects the rest of what the syringe has to offer into Alexis's vein. A powerful, euphoric high engulfs.

Hallucinations and delirium invade. Heroin and undiagnosed bipolar at play. The result, psychosis. It hits hard.

The One-in-Need slips away, into the darkness. Alexis regains connection with reality. The misguided trip shatters her psyche. Shame overtakes her disheartened spirit.

This is not who I am!

In her need to cleanse, Alexis decides everything touched by the One-in-Need must go! Possessions fly out the third story apartment window. Startled roommates stop Alexis before she flings her beloved Apple laptop below.

Alexis strips and gets into the shower. She scrubs forcibly to expunge demons encountered during the drug-induced flight. Unsuccessful, Alexis's exhausted body slides down the wet shower wall.

She slumps to a seated position. Water beats down. From deep within moans and cries uncontrollably escape.

Concerned roommates dry Alexis. They help her dress and load her into a car. The destination?

The hospital emergency room.

ADMISSION #1

Chapter 4

*A*t the hospital ER, Alexis fails to meet criteria for involuntary psychiatric admission. She is not suicidal nor a threat to others. Alexis surrenders to self-admission.

In the psychiatric unit, Alexis attends group therapy. She meets a college student who chopped and chopped her hair with dull scissors as Alexis had done in a highly agitated state. Alexis no longer feels so alone.

Sedation, balanced meals and a forced routine restore physical strength. Alexis experiences centering and feels a sense of security. All is clean, all is pure. The world is not so scary now.

But it is a world far removed. There is no signage that leads visitors through hospital corridors to the psych unit. One must ride a padded elevator; walk down an eerie silent hall; face a locked steel grey door. A keypad with a speaker next to the door intimidates.

State your name and the purpose of your visit. What is your relationship to the patient? Did you bring anything to give the patient?

Visitors, discouraged.

Those inside . . . banished, secreted, isolated.

BIPOLAR

Chapter 5

*I*n the psych unit at age twenty-two, Alexis is diagnosed: rapid cycling bipolar I. Two worlds crash within her, mania and depression. Highs and lows few know. Little rest between cycles.

Alexis is informed, while there is treatment for bipolar, there is no cure. No single pill. Lifestyle changes must be made.

She is told bipolar medications require constant monitoring. Dosage levels and combinations need adjustment on an individual basis. Medications powerful in the beginning may become ineffective.

Alexis must make room for frequent appointments. It will be necessary to supplement medication with therapy. She'll need individual therapy; group therapy; and periodic sessions with a psychiatrist to adjust medications.

~ ~ ~ *Behind the Curtain of Bipolar I* ~ ~ ~

Approximately fifty percent (50%) of bipolar patients fail to take their medications. Failure to take bipolar meds can have drastic consequences. Relapse, suicidal ideation and re-admission to a psychiatric hospital among them.

Yet, there are many reasons bipolar patients do not take their meds. Primarily, they may not realize they are sick. Their attitude may be one of rejection of illness; rejection of help; and rejection of medication.[1]

They may want to avoid mental illness stigma. Or, they may lose patience. It can take years, if not decades, of trial-and-error for an individual to find the right pharmaceutical combination.

Side effects on body, mind and spirit is another major cause of medication non-adherence. Meds may deflate the spirit, numb passion; flatten life. Excessive weight gain, tremors, nausea, gastric problems and decreased sexual function for the body. For the mind, slow thinking; a decrease in clarity; and difficulty with recall.

Many with bipolar I miss manic energy while on medication. Manic

---

[1]Amador, Xavier, *I Am Not Sick, I Don't Need Help! How to Help Someone with Mental Illness Accept Treatment*, 10th Anniv. ed (New York, 2011, Vida Press).

energy on which they depend to sustain careers, financial obligations and commitments. Commitments that go beyond themselves.

They may believe mania is essential. That, this time, willpower will be enough to keep mania in check; that medication will be unnecessary. However, churns, twists and swirls of bipolar I suddenly unleashed from medication pose a formidable challenge. A chaotic battle ground awaits.

Severe mood swings and emotional imbalance lurk in the shadows ready to reappear; suicidal thoughts, eager to re-emerge; all wait to inhabit a vulnerable, unmedicated mind.

If drugs and alcohol are abused in an effort to self-medicate, they may lead to substance abuse disorder (SUD) and possibly to substance-induced psychosis. When that happens, suicide risks escalate.

Bipolar must be carefully managed; but first and foremost,
the diagnosis of bipolar must be accepted.

FEAR

Chapter 6

*A*fter diagnosis, Alexis is in near panic: *"I don't want to be like dad!"* Her father had bipolar which was not carefully managed. It was misdiagnosed, mis-medicated, unmonitored.

What Alexis cannot internalize is, it was not bipolar, but its mismanagement that produced dangerous results. Mismanagement combined with something deeper: an internal rage. A rage that propelled him, while holding a loaded shotgun, to threaten her life, mine and his; a double-murder-suicide. Alexis underestimates the power of his darkened spirit to take him to places she would never go.

Alexis underestimates the power of *her* spirit to propel her. And propel her it would, if nurtured. Alexis's spirit, one of compassion, caring and giving.

Alexis wrongly equates sharing her father's bipolar diagnosis as determinative of a dark destiny for her. A destination Alexis fears; a destination she wants to flee. A destination her spirit would never entertain.

Alexis's fear infects her outlook. It paralyzes her ability to accept bipolar. It unnecessarily strips her of hope.

Alexis's fear of bipolar renders her situation perilous.

BREAK

Chapter 7

*A*lexis is discharged on heavy medications from the psych unit and returns to campus. Awkward silence greets. Her psychiatric condition goes largely unspoken.

Alexis is uncharacteristically behind on course work. It's her final semester. Term papers and honors projects are due.

She tries to complete a paper for a professor. A task that would have taken only a few hours, is now daunting. Her wings of mania clipped by medications, her passion muted, her spirit flattened. A stranger in her own life.

She tries to work long hours but lacks manic energy. Her brain will not engage in its usual rapid-fire sequence. Chemical alteration, sedation of her mind.

Alexis pushes hard. She wants to fulfill criteria to graduate as a Centennial Scholar. Her efforts are to no avail. She weakens. She contracts mono.

Alexis knows not how to cope. She requests medical leave. She is about to break from that which grounds her.

I fly to New York. I arrive with two large suitcases. Suitcases as empty as my awareness about the seriousness of bipolar. As empty as my knowledge about bipolar management.

Suitcases as empty as my knowledge of . . . what to do next.

OKLAHOMA

Chapter 8

While on medical leave at home in Oklahoma, Alexis tries to rest, but she is restless. She does not trust herself. She is uneasy. She does not want to be left alone.

Alexis follows me everywhere, to work and to bed. Strongly medicated, she is not comfortable with social interaction. She cannot drive and has no drive.

Other than an occasional smile, she is unrecognizable, even to me — her mother. She is locked within psychotropic medications. "Gun night" with her dad torments her.

Alexis sees a therapist and manages to restore some energy. Yet, she yearns to leave. Alexis finds no satisfaction, inspiration or camaraderie in Oklahoma. It's time to reconnect with a place that grounds her.

Not yet ready for New York City, we decide her older cousin Samantha's home in the Blue Ridge Mountains of North Carolina is the place to go. A place where she has her own bedroom. A safe place to embark on her journey to reengage and reenergize.

Loving extended family members will surround her. Alexis adores her young distant cousins who live next door, and they adore her. She has social ties.

Perhaps Alexis will resume a part
time job she held last year at a local coffee shop.

31

NORTH CAROLINA

Chapter 9

*I*n North Carolina, Alexis settles among the tranquil Blue Ridge
mountains. Yet, external calm fails to quell internal longings.
Peaceful surroundings fail to quiet strong desires.

Alexis aches for Barnard; quick thinking; the fast pace of New York
City. The stillness of a one stoplight town generates anxiety. Still water
awaiting a waterfall.

Alexis does not know how to handle slow living nor medicated,
muddled thinking. Her thoughts fade and vanish. Oh, if they could only
be captured. To be flooded with insights that erupt and multiply. How to
recapture, restore, reinvigorate that energy?

The medications must go!

Alexis begins with pills labeled antipsychotic.

I am not psychotic. I'm not taking this.

Abrupt cessation of antipsychotics leads to deep despair.

A despair that beckons death.

THE PLOT

Chapter 10

*A*lexis's emotional free-fall caused by sudden cessation of medicines, takes her to great depths. At the bottom of which she beckons death. Death fails to heed her call.

Alexis must go to it. She conceives a suicide plot. A loaded handgun in an unlocked safe in Sam's cabin writes the lines to Alexis's one act play.

Alexis carries the gun to Grandmother Geneva's neighboring cabin. A cabin Alexis went to as a child. A cabin now vacant.

Alexis walks to the back of the carport on its dank earthen floor. She sits atop an old trunk. She gazes out to a tire swing.

A tire swing her father once pushed. *Higher, higher!* Alexis and her little sister squeal in excitement as they try to touch their toes to the top of the carport in which Alexis now sits. Alexis's thoughts flash forward to when her father threatened her life. She considers fulfilling his imbedded death wish.

Alexis cannot go through with it. She bolts from the carport and into the thick dark undergrowth. Her feet follow the well-worn path back to Sam's. She ducks to avoid low hanging limbs. Her vision blurred by panicked tears.

In a time of duplicity, Alexis hands the gun to Sam. She confesses the plot to end life. Sam immediately drives Alexis to the town's primary care physician.

Sam is told to take Alexis to the county hospital.

ADMISSION #2

Chapter 11

*A*t the North Carolina county hospital, Alexis meets criteria for involuntary psychiatric care. She is a danger to herself. Once admitted, medications are restarted. Suicide's mission is thwarted.

Alexis goes to group therapy. There is no one of similar age. No one who shares stories to which she relates. No one with whom she bonds. No one in whom she trusts.

Alexis hears tales of abuse. Violent men who beat their wives. Men and women who abuse alcohol and drugs. Stories which break her most sensitive heart.

"Mom, this is like living in a truck stop."

One day my morning phone call from Alexis comes too early.

"Honey, why are you not at breakfast?"

"I don't feel like eating."

"Didn't anyone come for you?"

"No."

I fear she's being neglected; going under for the final time. Her condition precarious. No room to weaken. Too frail to falter.

Her physician recommends the hospital's working farm for psychiatric patients. I worry about a lack of supervision, inadequate treatment and a lack of trained personnel.

Alexis is hesitant.

TRANSFER

Chapter 12

I arrive to free my brilliant daughter from this rural North Carolina hospital. My plan? Transfer Alexis to a private mental health facility in Atlanta.

We stop at Sam's to get fresh clothing. The house is quiet. I step into the bathroom. Alexis rushes around the corner.

"Alexis? Alexis! Where are you going?"

I follow the small shadow cast by my oh-so-slim daughter. I find her sitting dejectedly on the wood floor of Sam's bedroom. She faces an open, empty safe.

I realize what she is doing. My heart sinks. I quietly ask:

"Alexis, is that where the gun was stored?"

"Yes."

She sulks out of the room. Frightened by what I just witnessed, my hands tremble as I quickly shove clothing into her large red suitcase.

"Alexis, get in the car."

I am apprehensive she will not, but she does. We leave. After about two hours, we are within an hour of Atlanta.

I pull into a *Chick-fil-A*. We go through the drive-thru. Alexis eats as if starved then turns towards me.

"Mom let's go to Costa Rica. Just you and me. Let's get away from all of this. *Please,* Mom."

With all my heart, I want to say yes, to take her away. Lamely I say, "I can't, honey."

"Why not, Mom?"

Her eyes look desperate, plaintively grasping for strength. Wanting me to fill her with hope and love.

"I have a job, I have your little sister, a house. I can't just go to Costa Rica. Besides your doctor didn't discharge you. She entered a transfer order."

Silence. Pause.

"Alexis, suicide is not an option."

"Why not, Mom? I don't want to do this anymore. I'm *done.*"

Medicated for several days now, her soul barely shines. Her light

47

dimmed. But she will not survive off meds where she will spin either dangerously high or low, bursting barriers not meant to be broken.

The only constant is her core. Her beautiful essence remains, clouded yet present. The person I love is always there. Never so far up nor so far fallen that my heart cannot sense hers.

". . . what if hell is the price to pay for suicide?" I worry aloud.

"Like that Robin Williams movie? I've watched it a hundred times. His wife goes to hell for killing herself and he has to go get her."

"Right . . . Alexis, I love you. I would miss you soo much. Suicide is not an option."

Tears flow.

ADMISSION #3

Chapter 13

W e arrive at the private Atlanta facility, park and slowly lumber arm-in-arm into the reception area. We are greeted and taken to a small conference room. It has clear acoustical walls and tile floors. There is no décor; nothing on the conference table.

A woman arrives with papers in hand, holding a pen. She goes over medical history with the two of us. I answer for Alexis, in the negative, to multiple diseases listed.

Alexis interrupts me.

"The answer is *Yes*. I have hepatitis C."

I look at her inquisitively.

"That's what they told me in New York."

The woman stands and asks Alexis to come with her. She ushers Alexis into an adjoining but smaller conference room. Clear walls separate us.

I watch but cannot hear. Alexis's demeanor lacks vigor, a defeated slump in her shoulders. She signs papers.

After a few minutes, another woman enters the room in which I wait. She sits in a chair next to me at the long bleak conference table. She goes over papers for me to sign.

She reassures me I am making no financial commitment. I am confused. I expect to pay. Alexis is my daughter.

"Alexis is an adult. She signs her own contract."

Alexis rejoins me. We sit alone for a few moments. We feel eyes upon us.

A physician enters the room. She introduces herself as Dr. Sarah Davis. Dr. Davis is a psychiatrist, a recent graduate of Duke University School of Medicine.

She appears warm and competent. I intuit we can trust her. It feels as if she is the safety net we've been seeking.

I tell Alexis to dig deep and really try to cooperate. Her doctor corrects me.

"Alexis is too depressed," I am calmly told, "to rationally think her way out of this. The last thing Alexis needs is to be told she can control this. She can't. What she needs," I am lightly scolded, "is not a pep talk but strong medication, rest, structure and therapy. Please just leave her with me."

It is late. I know not what else to do. I abide.

I check into a nearby hotel. I am exhausted. A sense that transferring Alexis was the right thing to do permeates my worry, brings relief.

A deep sigh softens my fall into sleep.

GOODBYE

Chapter 14

*T*he next morning, I return to hug Alexis goodbye as she embarks on treatment in Atlanta. I see her suitcase by the admissions desk, still zipped. I am told someone must search through it before Alexis can have it. I worry about what she is doing without her things.

I wait in a small room. Alexis is brought to me. She's wearing a hospital gown. Her escort leaves. Alexis collapses into my lap.

"I want to go back to that farm in North Carolina, Mom."

Alexis slings her arms around my neck in desperation.

"I told Dr. Davis I was scared in that other hospital because they use electric shock treatment," Alexis utters between gasps of tearful cries, "Afterwards, they'd wander the halls like hallow shells."

"What'd she say?"

"She said they use electric shock here, too! When patients get too depressed to eat, they *shock* them. Mom, I want to leave. I'll go to that farm. Please don't leave me here."

She tightens her grip around me.

"Alexis, you tried to get a gun yesterday. I cannot let you leave. We already transferred you."

"Mom, please!"

"Let's do what Dr. Davis says. I don't think you are well enough to live on that farm. I think Dr. Davis can help you. Let's give her a chance."

Alexis curls deep into me. Her frail frame presses against me.

"Please don't leave me here, Mom. *Please!*"

Dr. Davis enters the room. Alexis jumps back onto her chair. Dr. Davis surveys the situation.

"She'll be fine. I promise. Just leave us now. I know it's hard, but please just go."

Tears stream from Alexis, from me. I stand weak-kneed. I leave what is left of my daughter in the care of her physician.

I approach a locked glass door that leads into a small holding area blockaded by another glass door. I hear a loud buzz, then a click, as the door unlocks. Before I pass through the second door, I look back.

Alexis is standing in her beige hospital gown. Our eyes meet. She looks so lost, so broken, so alone. My heart breaks.

A nurse takes my tearful daughter by her thin arm and leads her past the nurses' station. I notice someone lying on a mattress on the floor. It seems odd, but I stay focused on Alexis.

My last vision of Alexis is in her pale gown, trembling, walking away. Away from honors classes, volunteer activities, helping others . . .

away from me.

DEATH WATCH

Chapter 15

*D*r. Davis and I talk on the phone. Alexis is losing weight. She's not eating, not communicating.

I call the nurses' station. I provide my authorization code. I wait and wait and wait on hold. Finally, I hear Alexis's meek voice.

"Hi, Mom."

". . . Alexis, Dr. Davis tells me you are not eating."

"Mom, would you eat turkey slices still frozen in the middle?"

"Alexis, if you lose one more pound, Dr. Davis is considering electric shock treatment."

That afternoon, flowers arrive from Sam. A nurse sets the vase on Alexis's bedside table. Alexis sees the glass vase as her way out.

Alexis shatters it. In rush nurses. They take Alexis from her room. She is relegated to a mattress on the floor next to the nurses' station.

Alexis is on suicide watch.

RUSH

Chapter 16

*T*he next time I talk with Alexis I can tell she flipped from suicidal depression to a frenetic pace. She is on a mission. A mission for release.

I hear terror in her voice.

"Mom, I have to get out of here! You have *got* to help me."

"Alexis, in order to get out, you have to let Dr. Davis help you. You have to engage in therapy. You can't just tell her you don't want to talk."

"Okay, Mom, I'll talk with her."

"And, you have to participate in group therapy."

"Okay, I'll go. What else?"

"Well, you have to eat."

"I will. I'll do anything. I just want out."

"Alexis, you will get out when you are better. But you have to choose to get better. Dr. Davis cannot do this alone."

"Okay. I want to, Mom. I'll do it. I'll get better."

RELEASE

Chapter 17

*A*lexis fulfills each of Dr. Davis's requirements. To her dismay, Dr. Davis still will not release her. Alexis calls me. There's desperation, exasperation in her voice.

"Why won't she let me out? I'll just leave AMA — against medical advice. I've heard people talk about it."

"Alexis, you can't just leave."

"Why not, Mom?"

"Alexis, Dr. Davis will discharge you, but only after post-discharge plans are in place."

Alexis uses her calling card. She contacts her North Carolina therapist. They schedule individual therapy appointments. Together, they find a group therapy program and a psychiatrist to oversee prescriptions. Alexis makes transportation arrangements. She fulfills each discharge criteria.

Alexis is to be released.

DISCHARGE

Chapter 18

*B*efore Alexis leaves, Dr. Davis gives her discharge instructions. Dr. Davis first goes over Alexis's medications. She tells Alexis she is discharging her on the highest level of the most powerful medications available.

Alexis's medications again include an antipsychotic. Dr. Davis goes over side-effects. She explains:

"Alexis, these medications may lead to severe weight gain, including the possibility of obesity and ultimately diabetes. The antipsychotics may cause tremors. You must, however, stay on all prescribed medications until a physician deems it safe to reduce them."

Alexis hears *severe weight gain . . . obesity . . . diabetes.* Her mind freezes. She cannot imprint those onto herself, her life, her body.

Dr. Davis then addresses lifestyle changes. "Alexis, you must reduce stress; simplify your life; stay on medication; and attend therapy."

Alexis interprets Dr. Davis's instructions as: *You can no longer navigate college life in New York City, fulfill rigorous academic demands, work part-time, and participate in multiple causes. Rather, you must give up your dreams, tranquilize your mind and mute your passions.* Alexis's sense of purpose and connection to that which inspires, motivates, ignites her slips away.

Alexis can no longer visualize a future she desires.

MOUNTAIN HOME

Chapter 19

S am arrives at the facility and parks in the circle drive. Alexis steps onto the front walkway. She squints. It's the first time in almost two weeks she's been outdoors.

Alexis feels groggy and a little weak. She slowly gets into Sam's car. Sam drives northeast along tree lined Georgia highways.

After about two hours they turn onto a two-lane highway that winds through mountains, going in and out of Georgia and North Carolina. Curves, small farms and serenity fill Alexis's eyes. She rolls down her window. Cool spring air inhabits her lungs.

Silence eventually fills the car. Alexis leans against the passenger door. Music replaces silence. Her head full of music, her body warmed by sun, her lungs filled with fresh air; Alexis drifts asleep.

Sam slowly turns onto a narrow blacktop that leads to her mountain home. Alexis raises heavy eyelids. Six-foot rhododendron hedges come into focus.

Sam turns onto her private drive. Mountain laurel bushes crowd the lane. Azalea buds hold moist flowers awaiting spring release.

Sam and Alexis unload the car. They sit on a back wood deck elevated over a stream. Multiple bird feeders surround them.

Small tufted titmouse birds flit from branch to branch. They swoop down and hop along the deck railing. They joyfully whistle their song and leave with a sunflower seed in their beak.

In times of silence, water is heard splashing over rocks blocking its determined path. A deep breath absorbs moisture from the stream. A slight aroma lifts from a nearby tulip magnolia tree.

The hope of renewal is in the air.

SPRING

Chapter 20

*I*n this dawning of spring, when others are infused with hope, unfulfilled dreams weigh heavily on Alexis. Graduation announcements addressed but not sent. Fittings for a gown not worn. A graduation cap meant to be tossed among cheers sits in dark silence. Gold chords for graduation with honors lay in an unopened box.

Alexis grieves the loss of her beloved college and all of its promise. The loss of being with her graduating class. The loss of plans.

Alexis is fearful. Fearful of another psychiatric admission, looming medical bills. Fearful of memory loss from electric currents running through her brain. Fearful of being like her dad.

Spring is a common time for suicide. Not winter, when depressed souls go unnoticed. But spring, where misery and dread are in stark contrast to hope and new beginnings.

Spring, where the depressed feel they do not belong.

OFF TRACK

Chapter 21

Still on medical leave from Barnard, Alexis attends an extended family dinner. A long brightly colored table filled with berries blue and red; brown crusted bread; vegetables orange and yellow; black and green olives and so much more. Welcoming hugs exchanged.

Alexis sits at the long wood plank dining table next to Julia, Sam's mother. Alexis so admires Julia. Across the table sits June, Julia's long-time friend.

Julia and June share stories. All join in laughter about practical jokes the two played in days gone by. Alexis gently asks, "June, would you please pass the cheese plate?"

"You mean *Julia*? You said June!"

Everyone laughs. Alexis sinks with knowledge she is dulled by medication. She feels derailed.

That evening, Alexis calls me. She tells of her embarrassment in confusing Julia and June's names.

"Oh, sweetheart, it sounds as if it was a fleeting moment. Don't dwell on it."

"I'm not, Mom. I just can't think on all this medication . . . Mom, I should be getting ready for graduation."

"I know, honey . . . you know, many students miss a semester or change majors and need extra time to finish college. You are not so far off track."

Alexis feels so very far off track.

REALIZATION

Chapter 22

*T*he next morning is Easter Monday, 2006. Alexis awakens with a tremor in her hands. She feels nauseous. Her mind foggy. Her favorite ring will barely slip over her puffy finger. Complications now real; no longer an abstract concept.

Her body and mind highjacked, no longer hers. Invaded by prescription chemicals. And yet, every day she must fill her palm with pills and swallow. She is to repeatedly ingest that which makes her feel physically ill, shaky, bloated; slows her mind; and, mutes her soul.

Alexis's first post-discharge therapy appointment is in a few hours. Alexis goes to the closet to choose an outfit. She looks through her modest, yet exotic, wardrobe pieced together while living in New York.

A wardrobe that may soon no longer fit.

THERAPY

Chapter 23

*A*lexis wants to go to her first post-discharge therapy appointment with her North Carolina therapist, Karen. Alexis has seen her intermittently since the summer before starting college. She wants to go to therapy but trembling hands concern: *Should I drive?*

Alexis recalls driving three days earlier, just after returning from Atlanta, to locate the meeting place for group therapy. She had no problems with the twenty-minute drive each way from her mountain home. Her driving concerns diminish.

Alexis leaves early so not to rush. So not to pass on the narrow two-lane mountain roads. She arrives at Karen's office ahead of schedule.

Karen welcomes Alexis with a loving presence. Alexis tells Karen about locating the place for group therapy. She lists her medications and dosages. Karen asks Alexis to describe how the medications affect her.

Alexis tells Karen about the difficulty thinking clearly and the nausea. She holds her trembling puffy hands out for Karen's observation. Karen reassures Alexis she will convey these side effects to the psychiatrist overseeing prescriptions.

Alexis turns to tomorrow. She and her father's cousin Zach have a meeting scheduled to go over medications. Zach is a local pharmacist who manages his own pharmacy. He will explain each medication, in detail, to Alexis.

Karen knows Zach and is encouraged by positive steps Alexis is taking to accept her diagnosis and medications. She compliments Alexis on the progress she is making. Karen senses Alexis's determination.

Karen is very fond of Alexis. She would never let Alexis drive if she didn't believe it safe. Alexis and Karen confirm their next scheduled session.

Karen writes something on a piece of paper. She folds it and slips it into Alexis's hand. Alexis gets into her borrowed car.

She settles behind the wheel. With trembling hands, Alexis unfolds the piece of paper. She reads what Karen wrote.

I am healing. I need time. I will get better.

RECKLESSNESS

Chapter 24

*A*lexis sits in the car with many questions, doubts and fears. So few answers. No matter what she does or how well she does it, bipolar will always be with her.

Alexis knows not how to look past the moment. She knows not how to visualize life after medication reduction; after individual and group therapy for bipolar; and, with lifestyle changes. She cannot grasp adjustment and acceptance.

Anxious, Alexis turns the small car towards Sam's cabin. She turns up the music. Alexis accelerates as she tops one hill, then another. Speed liberates.

Over the next hill a blind curve awaits. Alexis steers left. No shoulder. The roadway recently resurfaced. A three inch drop off. Her right front tire falls into soft ground.

Alexis pulls the steering wheel hard to the left. Her right front tire digs a sideways rut into the ground as it fights roadway's edge. No guardrail between Alexis and the mountain's steep embankment.

Terrified, she struggles to get her car back under control. Finally, her front tire hops back onto the road's surface. Her steering wheel still turned to the left. The light-weight car veers across the center line.

An oncoming 18-wheeler rounds the curve. The semi swerves hard right. Little shoulder. Nine wheels rise off the roadway and screech along the side of the abutting mountain. Nowhere to go.

The crush of metal is heard miles away. EMTs having lunch at a nearby roadside café recognize the horrific sound. They rush to the scene.

They arrive within minutes.

TRANSCENDENCE

Chapter 25

Zach, returning from an appointment, drives the same mountain road traveled by Alexis. He tops a hill and sees a long row of red brake lights ahead. He slows to a stop.

A sheriff walks down the line of stopped cars. Zach rolls down his window. Sheriff McGill leans in to speak to Zach. They recognize each other.

Besides being a pharmacist, Zach is a multi-black belt karate instructor. He volunteers for night shifts on the rescue squad. He works with law enforcement and medical personnel to help rescue stranded hikers or drivers who run off the road.

"Well, hello there, Zach. There has been a very bad accident ahead. We are diverting traffic. You will have to turn around and use a different route."

Zach is familiar with the sharp curve over the next hill. No guard rails. The scene of prior accidents.

He pulls off the road and waits for an opportunity to make a U-turn. As he waits, his front windshield is inundated with orange and black butterflies. Zach is puzzled. Monarchs migrate in fall, not spring.

The mysterious butterflies swarm his car. Zach watches in awe as they form a cloud and swirl towards the sun. Zach is awash with a sense of peace. A feeling he often receives from Alexis.

He thinks of Alexis but knows not why.

OVERCORRECTION

Chapter 26

*T*he next day, Zach talks with investigating officers. They give him full access to their reports. The collision is classified as an accident.

Zach returns to the scene to do his own investigation. He safely parks and walks along the extended sideways rut dug by Alexis's front right tire. He determines Alexis did all she could to get her car back on the roadway. A classic overcorrection. Zach agrees, it was an accident.

Off to the side of the road, a white piece of paper flutters in the breeze. Zach walks to it. He disentangles it. There's handwriting on it. He picks it up.

I am healing. I need time. I will get better.

Zach's eyes fill with tears.

REMEMBRANCES

Chapter 27

*T*he *Columbia Daily Spectator* again runs a front-page story about Alexis. The article describes her as a well-known campus face. Several who knew Alexis express remembrances:

❖ *. . . Lexie was an engaged and active member of our community and a strong student leader on many important issues . . .*

❖ *I think she put her whole heart into whatever she undertook . . .*

❖ *Lexie was a very intelligent and involved student who worked to make the world a better place, particularly through feminist activism . . .*

❖ *She was involved in everything but always wanted to make sure everyone else was taken care of . . .*

RISE, LEXIE, RISE

Chapter 28

*E*veryone is shocked. She was so young; involved in so many activities; so passionate; so alive; so accomplished. All are heartbroken. One life, three services.

In Oklahoma City, a traditional service is held at the downtown Episcopal cathedral. White lilies from Easter fill the church. The priest speaks beautifully about Alexis's struggles. She refers to Alexis's bipolar.

In North Carolina, the local paper runs a front-page article with an accompanying radiant photo of Alexis. Alexis is described eloquently. The news of her death shocks. Many gather for a tear-filled service. Heartfelt stories, poems and some laughter are shared.

Following the service, loved ones gather around moss covered headstones at the hillside family cemetery. The urn holding Alexis's ashes is lovingly placed between her great-great-great grandparents' headstones. Blooming redbud and dogwood trees, anchored by purple hyacinths, exude serenity.

In New York, Alexis's classmates hold a campus celebration of life attended by professors, mentors and students. They serve Alexis's favorite — chocolate covered strawberries. Her classmates establish the *Alexis Knox Internship Fund*. A fund to pay a stipend to Barnard students who otherwise could not financially afford to accept unpaid internships.

The generally reclusive feminist icon, Ms. Gloria Steinem, so touched by Alexis's passionate yet ethereal spirit, attends the service. Ms. Steinem and others beautifully inscribe the guestbook.

Rise, Lexie, Rise!

. . . and may you rise with Ballasted Wings.

WHY THAT DAY

Chapter 29

*T*en years later, a burly police officer sitting on the front row of *Crisis Intervention Training* (CIT) raises his hand. I call upon him as part of the Q&A following my family panel talk. I had spoken of Alexis's mental illness outcome. He asks: *"Why that day?"*

I have no answer. I go home to write. I research. I find that mania is associated with high risk-taking, impulsive, reckless conduct. During mania, there is a lack of foresight; little planning; disregard of long-term goals. Compulsions go unchecked.

Suicide may occur during mania, but chances may be highest during a mixed episode. A mix of manic and depressive features, perhaps when transitioning from one cycle to the next. A dangerous co-mingling; an overlap of cycles that should not cross.

Alexis experienced rapid cycling between mania and depression. Did depressive thoughts mix with a manic surge? Rise on manic flames? Were suicidal thoughts ignited by manic fire?

The term "suicide" confers blame-shifting, death shaming: *There was nothing we could do. It was what she wanted. It was her choice; a selfish act.*

"Suicide" also bestows shame and blame onto those on the inside: *Weren't there warning signs? Did you not see it coming?*

Suicide is a powerful word. But not powerful enough to embody a complex mind. Not powerful enough to infuse reason into a brain laden with misfires. Not powerful enough to penetrate clarity into murky water.

Whatever the death label, suicide or recklessness, how to answer the question: *"Why that day?"* With ambiguity? *She had an accident with a truck as it rounded a blind curve on a narrow mountain road as her high-speed car flew out of control. However, she had just been released from her third psychiatric confinement. Before that third inpatient admission, Alexis pronounced: "I'm done."*

Or, with an answer which encompasses complex neural circuitry? *A bipolar reward circuitry that favors high-risk taking. A circuitry that fails to quell impulsivity.*

Or, should the question be answered with simplicity? *She wasn't happy. She didn't like what her future held. She lacked hope.*

Can hope transcend all? At some point, we accept hope cannot transcend physical illnesses like cancer run rampant. Must we accept that bipolar, too, may render hope impotent?

There is a plethora of mental illnesses with which bipolar may mix: social anxiety disorder; generalized anxiety disorder; panic disorder; post-traumatic stress disorder; obsessive compulsive disorder; and psychotic disorder.

When multiple mental illnesses combine, their power can exceed coping skills; concoct a lethal cocktail. In the presence of multiple mental illnesses, suicidal ideations and behavior may increase.

It seems clear, there is no single answer to: *"Why that day?"* Multiple factors come into play. Each factor individually contributes to the outcome, as does the cumulative effect.

So, why blame, judge, scorn? Why infer weakness, cowardice and selfishness on those who die as a result of complex mental illnesses? Why not empathy?

Alexis died that day because
mental illness exceeded her coping skills.

BIPOLAR LINKS

Chapter 30

*A*s coping skills can be enhanced through connections and resources that promote and build resilience, I decided to end Alexis's cautionary tale by pulling together bipolar resources that support bipolar resilience. There were too many links for a book chapter. I decided to create *BipolarLinks.com*.

BipolarLinks's Mission is to: 1) help remove fear and uncertainty after a bipolar diagnosis; 2) instill understanding, options and belonging; and 3) provide resources, tools and empowerment. It is a gateway to bipolar resources.

BipolarLinks is a bipolar resource hub. Through its many links, help is available to answer questions regarding bipolar like:

What now? What's next? What can I expect?

GRATITUDE

Chapter 31

*I*n the final days before submission of *Ballasted Wings: Why That Day?* for publication, I received the list of young women who, during the 2018-2019 academic year, received stipends from the *Alexis Knox Internship Fund.* The list of unpaid internships in which they participated was impressive. The young women were impressive.

I was overcome with gratitude. Gratitude for the Barnard memorial fund; for the impact Alexis's short life had on so many; for her story being told. I felt gratitude that her story, as well as her life, lead to action: the creation of *BipolarLinks.com* and the *Alexis Knox Internship Fund.*

Gratitude that the positive impact of Alexis's life would continue to be a force for change. A force to empower those affected by bipolar, and to empower young Barnard women. A book born in grief evolved into a book published in gratitude.

> *". . . practicing gratitude invites joy into our lives."*
> —*Dr. Brené Brown*

WHAT IF

Chapter 32

What if . . . Alexis and I understood bipolar was not a gift to be exploited? That bipolar was not a free set of wings on which to soar, accomplish, ride? But rather, something to be carefully managed?

What if manic sails could be pushed with a steady wind? *What if* one pill addressed bipolar I symptoms as is advertised today? *What if* Alexis received trauma therapy and was diagnosed before she spun dangerously out of control with overcommitments and deadly lows? Spun into psychosis and the hands of death?

What if the *Active Minds* on-campus exhibit visited Barnard and Alexis saw all the empty silent backpacks symbolizing the many students who lost their lives to suicide? Would that have dramatically impacted her? Would she have vowed to never let that happen to her?

What if she had been supported by online communities and groups like *Polar Warriors, bpHope, The Mighty, BringChange2Mind* (BC2M), *JED* or *Active Minds*? Or, if Barnard College/Columbia University had been a JED Campus like it is today? Or, if post-hospitalization she entered the *Columbia Day Program* to keep her in Barnard, balanced and on track?

What if Alexis received treatment in a residential healing community like *CooperReiis? CooperReiis,* located in North Carolina close to where Alexis was, offers multifaceted treatment for mental health conditions like bipolar. It has transitional living options and offers an opportunity to take college level courses.

What if Alexis was cared for in programs designed for young adults like *Compass or Pathfinder* at Menninger Clinic? *What if* she received skills-based therapies on bipolar management? Received guidance on how to create her own path to bipolar resilience?

What if she received cognitive behavioral therapy (CBT) to help with self-acceptance and "change-acceptance?" Would dialectical behavior therapy (DBT), validation, phone coaching, and mindfulness have helped? How about eye movement desensitization and reprocessing (EMDR) to counteract PTSD? Or, interpersonal and social rhythm therapy (IPSRT) to improve mood awareness and medication adherence?

What if Alexis had gone to a *Promises Treatment Center* and had *The Daring Way*™ program as a part of her treatment? *The Daring Way*™ is based on Dr. Brené Brown's research. It reveals interconnection between vulnerability and courage; between worthiness and shame; and, builds resilience. Would Alexis have made a commitment to be alive, brave, and seen; become more resilient?

What if she accepted her diagnosis and not feared and run away from it? *What if* she embraced bipolar as a springboard for a career as a mental health advocate? Seen the great need as set forth by *BC2M* and felt the encouragement of *Active Minds*?

What if she read her original poetry at a *This Is My Brave* event or became a successful blogger for *The Mighty* or *bpHope*? Perhaps had a goal of one day giving a speech at a *NAMI National Convention*? Been received with applause and support? Felt the enriching, inspiring, purposeful gratification of helping others release fears, dreams and hopes?

What if she developed a rewarding career with *Mental Health America* (MHA), *International Bipolar Foundation* (IBPF), *The Jed Foundation*, *Active Minds*, *BC2M*, *Depression and Bipolar Support Alliance* (DBSA) or *World Health Organization* (WHO)? Or, perhaps with a diversified organization who had a place for a mental health reporter/advocate/speaker? Or, with a proactive government entity like the *Substance Abuse and Mental Health Services Administration* (SAMHSA)?

What if she saw bipolar as a way to a life of purpose and meaning? *What if* she attended a DBSA support group and saw a future role for herself as a peer-support leader? Grew and transformed her experiences into empathy and compassion for others; become an activist for eliminating mental health stigma?

Alexis would have been a powerful force as a mental health advocate . . . *if only* she had accepted bipolar, found support and guidance needed to build bipolar resilience, bipolar ballast. Instead of feeling she did not belong, she felt *bipolar strong?*

What if Alexis was transferred to a psychoeducation program after stabilization rather than discharged to her own resources? Would she have found what is described in her last email username:

Ballasted Wings?

AFTERWORD

Patients hospitalized for unanticipated serious physical events often enter post-acute care programs. In such interim programs, patients and support persons receive education about the physical condition. Self-care best practices and condition management are taught.

Patients hospitalized for serious psychiatric disorders, such as bipolar, are commonly discharged without the benefit of a post-acute care psychoeducation program. Through education, psychiatric patients learn episode warning signs and common triggers. Psychoeducation develops internal coping skills and knowledge of external resources. Psychoeducation about the condition and its treatment significantly increases the willingness to stay on bipolar medications and lowers the risk of relapse.

Perhaps this lack of post-acute care education and connection to resources accounts for the deplorable *increased* short-term risk of suicide associated with psychiatric hospitalization. Being discharged with such an increased suicide risk is *beyond* unacceptable. It must end.

Why Not Today?

WEBSITES

BallastedWings.com

BipolarLinks.com